Endors(

Untether My Heart – A Poetic Gem!
After a series of near-death experiences and powerful Heaven encounters, God started to move and capture Charmaine's heart in a deeper way than she ever expected.

He drew her to a place of total abandonment, from focusing on the daily workings of this world, to untether her heart into God's mysteries and love.

Richard Fellows - B.App. Theol. Author and Teacher.

Written straight from the heart of God.
It is with great joy and delight that I endorse this beautiful book of poetry. It is filled with wonderful words of encouragement and hope.

I believe this has been written straight from the heart of God and one cannot help but be greatly encouraged.

Charmaine has been given a beautiful gift and I'm so thankful she is willing to share it with others.

Rev Julie Calvert - National Director – Healing Rooms NZ.

A Truly Remarkable Collection of Heaven/God Inspired Poetry.
Untether My Heart is a well spring of words hidden deep in the heart of my sister Charmaine.

In 2020, a very dedicated intercessory prayer group was established called 'I once was blind, but now I see'. Over the 3-years that followed, a deeper revelation and love for Jesus burst into every part of our lives. The untapped well of poems came out like rays of sunshine, bursting through daily.

You will be moved and inspired as you read the poems in this book. I am blessed and honoured beyond words to

endorse this collection of heavenly inspired poems.
Helen Herbert – Pastor - New Beginnings Church - Kaeo.

These word-tapestries embody the very heart, emotion, and truth of God. Charmaine has miraculously captured life from Heaven.
It is my honour to endorse this book for Charmaine. Everything that is received from Heaven by the Spirit of God releases Heaven into the earth, and these poems are definitely filled with gems from on high. These verses are masterfully woven together to bring life, hope and healing into our many, needy, earthly experiences.
They are as balms that uplift and nourish the spirit, soul, and body towards health, peace, life, and abundance.
May the Lord infuse life into you through the words of this heavenly book.
Jason Cobb – The Life Foundation

Untether My Heart

Spelling is based on New Zealand English.

ISBN: 978-0-473-68633-8 (p/b)
ISBN: 978-0-473-68635-2 (Kindle)
ISBN: 978-0-473-68634-5 (ePub)

New Zealand
www.kinandkingdomsbooks.com

Publisher: Kin & Kingdoms Books.
Cover Design: Angela Curtis.

I Dedicate This Book To

Jesus my Saviour.

The lover of my soul
who walked with me through heartache
and so many trials.
Forever grateful.
Jesus, forever Yours.

Forward

The day before New Zealand went into lockdown (Covid) in 2020, Charmaine looked out of her lounge and saw two huge hands close her ranch sliders and heard the Lord speak.

"You're not going to lock down. I'm locking you in."

As each day and night came to a close, Charmaine was woken up around 2-3am every morning with a word from the Lord which she wrote down. Cryptic words of revelation unfolded into beautiful poems as the days went by. The Lord locked her in to unlock her heart! Aloneness is the 'Key' to His heart.

The Lord is good to those who wait for Him,
to the soul who seeks Him.
It is good that one should hope and wait quietly
for the salvation of the Lord.
Let him sit alone and keep silent,
because God had laid it on him."
Lamentations 3:25, 26, 28 (NKJV)

In the poems that follow, one is taken on a journey of Kingdom insights only found when we are called away to spend time alone with the Lord. Be encouraged as you read this book and let your heart grasp and appreciate the little things, the simple things, the treasures, and blessings God has for us. They are all around us in creation. Stop and ponder His heartbeat and hear His voice in frequencies of these revelational poems.

Richard Fellows - B.App. Theol. Author and Teacher.

Author's Note

Some time ago, I was at a church function. Not long after worship, I suddenly felt unwell. I went to my sister Helen to ask her to pray for me and I fell at her feet. She told me she believed I'd had a stroke. I was rushed to the hospital and had tests done, and yes, it was a full-on stroke. I was given the clot buster drug and then taken upstairs to the stroke ward.

Not long after, the Lord took me into a Heaven encounter. I arrived in a garden. It was so beautiful I can still remember every vivid detail.

It was like an old Roman garden with big pillars in each corner that were flanked by two long marble stools. There were towering trees on each side of the pillars. One had white blossoms and the other had big, pink flowers.

The colours of all the flowers and plants in the garden were so beautiful and much brighter than any I've seen on earth.

While I was standing there taking it all in, I saw Jesus walking towards me. I couldn't believe it. I was going to meet my King! I hadn't met Jesus like this before, but I knew deep within that it was Him. We walked around the garden together in silence. Not one word was spoken, but His love that flowed over me said all I needed to know.

Once we got back to where we started, Jesus looked at me and spoke.

"Come to the secret place for it's at the secret place Hidden treasures flow."

Then I woke up, and my life has never been the same. It wasn't long after I arrived home that poems started to flow from Heaven.

My prayer is that as you read, you will gain a greater intimacy with the Father. That like me, through these poems your heart will be untethered, and you'll be released into a new season where you too will experience the love of our Father.

This is my journey.

Charmaine

ADORATION

Jesus Is Alive

There's a gathering of the people
stirring in our land.
A shaking of the spirit
as He raises up His hand.
There's a hunger in the people
to see the King of Kings.
He is the hope of glory
who's come to set us free.
There are hearts being healed
because they have believed.
Jesus Christ has risen,
He's won the victory.

Father's Love

Father, You are my first
conversationin the morning,
and the last one at night.
You're the beginning of my day,
in the darkness,
You're my light.
You're a shield that surrounds me
to keep me safe from harm.
You cover me in Your love
and hold me in Your arms.
I will praise You, Father,
until the end of my days.
Then I will lean back against You,
and there I'll always stay.
I'll always remain
in my Father's arms.

Your Love is All I See

Your love is all I see.
Your gaze is fixed on me.
Your love is never ending.
Your love covers me.
You will never leave me.
You will never forsake me.
Your love is all I ever want to see.

True Love

Take me to the secret place
where I first met Your love.
You touched my heart and changed my life
from Heaven up above.
Your love is true,
Your love is pure.
No other love will do.
Your love fills me,
it completes me.
I love to be with You.

Jesus My Saviour

Jesus, a man of so much power
who walked in love and grace.
Wherever He would go
miracles would take place.
He walked in signs and wonders,
He did miracles everywhere.
Wherever Jesus went, children were always there.
He often spoke in riddles
to see if we could see.
To look beyond our natural eyes so
we would then believe.
His time on earth was short,
He changed so many lives.
Then one day it arrived,
and He became our sacrifice.
Because of His great love
He gave His life for all,
So, whoever would believe,
will not endure the fall.
He holds the keys of Hades for all eternity,
He died upon the cross so,
we could be set free.
He sits on the right side of His Father,
the King upon the throne.
We are all His children,
His beloved, His very own.

Before The Beginning Of Time

Your word say's nothing is impossible for You.
You clear our paths
and make them straight,
You turn everything up the right way.
In the chaos of our lives,
Your light removes all darkness.
You pursue us with everlasting love.
You never leave us or forsake us.
You planned everything for us
before the beginning of time.
Because we were already in Your heart,
Your love is pure, divine.

Loving Arms

I'm sitting in Your presence,
soaking in Your love.
How beautiful You are,
I just can't get enough.
Sitting in Your presence
is everything to me.
I'm abiding in Your loving arms
where I will always be.

Creator of All Things

Heaven and earth were formed in Your hands.
You speak, and it becomes.
By Your Word it is done.
Your every breath springs forth into life.
Your voice shakes the earth,
Your touch changes everything.
You breathed on us
and gave us life,
You made us in Your image,
in Your likeness.
You've given us everything
and held back nothing from us.
Your love is overflowing,
An ever-growing bliss.

Made New

In Your presence
I am made new.
The old has gone,
the new has come,
a new creation has now begun.
Here in Your presence, I am free,
no holding back all You've given to me.
I am in You,
and You are in me.
In Your presence I am whole,
no longer afraid,
now I am bold.
Here in Your presence,
I am redeemed,
saved by my Saviour for all to see.
Covered in the blood
of the spotless Lamb,
a child of God is who I am.
In Your presence
I am made new.

Name Above All Names

The name above of all names,
You never change,
You stay the same.
I'm holding on to Your presence
and I won't let go.
You are the life that fills my soul,
and the joy that makes me whole.
I will wait to hear Your voice
in the chaos and the noise.
I will be still and know
that You are God.
The King of kings
who reigns on high.

I See You

I see You in the morning,
I see You in the night.
I see You in my dark times,
I see You when it's light.
I see You in my trials,
I see You in my joy.
I see you in all things,
I see you King of Kings
and Lord of all.

Saviour of the World

Amazing love You have for us,
no words can mere man say.
The suffering You endured on that final day.
The pain Your body must have felt,
no words can we explain.
The crown of thorns forced on Your head,
the start of so much pain.
The nails driven through Your hands,
again, again, and again.
Six long hours past that day,
as darkness filled the land.
Then with a loud voice
You gave up Your spirit,
and the suffering met its end.
A violent earthquake shook the earth,
an angel from Heaven came down.
"Do not be afraid,"
He said to Mary.
"His garments here laid down.
Jesus Christ the sacrifice
has risen, He's not here.
Jesus Christ the perfect love
that cast's out all your fear."

My Life is Complete

How can my mind describe the way
I feel about You?
But to say
"My heart sings to You
because of all You do.
My hopes and dreams can now come true,
Father I am fully covered by You.
Jesus, the lover of my soul,
You gave Your life for mine
and now I am made whole.
Your love is sweet, sweet wine.
When I taste and see how sweet it is,
it simply blows my mind.
Your love is sweet love,
unending, unchanging.
It's Your love, Your pure love,
that makes me whole."

Breath of God

Let the knowledge of Your Son
come take over me.
Breath of God I welcome You,
Holy Spirit,
wind of God,
blow on us
and set us free.
You are the One
who opens the eyes of our hearts,
so, come breathe on us again.
Let the River of Life flow in our hearts,
our minds, our bodies, and souls.
Jesus, captivate our hearts
with the fullness of Your love.

The Secret Place

Jesus, take me to the Secret Place
where we can be alone.
Where we can talk of secret things
and I can have You on my own.
My heart's desire is to walk with You,
to have You call me friend.
To come into the Secret Place
where our time will never end.

Holy Spirit

Holy Spirit,
You have filled my heart.
Your sweet, sweet Spirit
has filled my every part.
I belong to You, Jesus,
caught up in Your amazing love.
Overwhelmed by Your goodness
and Heaven up above.
My soul rests in Your gentleness,
my life is in Your hands.
I surrender to Your will my King,
and will walk in all Your plans.

Above All Else

Above all else
I surrender to You, my King,
My heart is open to Your word,
to trust You and believe.
Your presence is overwhelming me,
I bow and worship thee.
Above all else,
Above all else,
I surrender to You, my King.

You Are There

I look to the heavens
and You are there.
I look to earth
and You are there.
I look at the people
and You are there.
I look in the mirror
and You are there.
You are the creator of all things
and you are everywhere.

He Paid the Price

You gave up Your crown,
You laid it down
to walk on unholy ground.
You did not judge
the things You saw,
but poured out Your love
more and more.
You healed the sick,
the lost, and unclean.
You came to save humanity.
You paid the price of sin and death
to set the captives free.
Jesus my heart remains forever Yours,
Yours completely.

My Heart Is Yours

My heart is Yours
every part of me.
Your love overwhelms me.
Oh, how You give it so freely.
Your amazing love,
You give completely.
My heart is Yours,
my hope is found in You,
My trust is too.
My heart is remains forever Yours.

You Take My Breath Away

I've never known a love
that would mean so much.
That I would long for
Your very touch.
A love that takes all fear away
and shines through the darkest day.
Your peace fills me
and covers me completely.
Jesus, you take my breath away.

Here I Am

Here I am
with all my heart,
forgiven, loved and free.
Thankful for Your amazing gift,
the love You've given me.
You are always here,
You never leave,
always by my side.
You call me yours,
Your beloved,
and because of Your amazing love,
I am Your spotless bride.

Face To Face

I'm sitting in my sister's room
overwhelmed by our great love.
Singing to my Saviour
in Heaven up above.
Your presence is so strong,
I'm in awe of Your amazing grace.
I long to be with You, Jesus,
kanohi ki te kanohi,
face to face.

Jesus Took My Sin

Jesus came and took my sin
and carried all the blame.
He took my loss
and deep despair
and took it as His own.
He carried it all away
on that dreadful day.
He willingly paid the price
for all that was lost.
The mocking, the beating,
the crown of thorns,
He took it all to the cross.
He came as a man,
the spotless Lamb,
the only Son of God.
The love of the Father,
the love of the Son,
the sacrifice
given for us.

Thank You

I am in awe of You Jesus.
You took me who had nothing
and turned me into something beautiful.
You gave me hope to believe
anything is possible with You.
You slowly spoke into my life
and filled me with a love unknown.
You showed me the path you made for my life
long before time began.
You gently pursued
and guided me
to walk with You all my days,
I don't have words to say
how grateful I am that you chose me.
Thank you will never be enough,
but with all my heart I say thank You.
With all my mind I say thank You,
With all my soul I say thank You.

I Lay Me Down

I lay me down with all my cares
and give my all to You.
I offer up my deepest thoughts,
my heart I give to You.
My hopes and dreams
so full of life
are now to be set free.
Jesus You are the air I breathe,
Your presence is inside of me,
my Saviour and my King.

I Want to See

I want to see what You can see,
The me You created me to be.
Chosen, forgiven,
cleansed and free.
To be with You for eternity.
The Holy One before me,
the righteous Son of the living God.
My beloved who to calls me.

Just One Look

Just one look
and everything changes.
I thought I knew what love was
until I met You.
I thought I knew it all
until I met You.
I thought life was good
until I met You.
Now I am whole
because I met you.
All it took was just one look.

On My Knees

Mountains so high
and valleys so low.
On my knees
is where I will always go.
I give to You
what's in my heart,
and wait for You
to make my path.
Lead me Jesus
and I will follow.
Call my name
and I will come.
Fill my heart
with Your pure love,
the love that
is more than enough.

You Know Me

Father God, You know me.
You know everything about me.
You know every detail.
Nothing is hidden from You.
You created me in the secret place
long before time began.
You carried me
in Your heart,
You made me
in Your image
and in your likeness.
Until the appointed time
of my life's great explosion,
You lavished your love on me.
I am loved,
pure and clean before You.
I am Your child.
I am the daughter of
the Almighty God and King.

He's Worthy

How do you start your day?
Do you go to the feet of Jesus
and ask Him to have His way?
Do you thank Him
for His amazing love
each and every day?
Do you sit there in the silence
and wait for Him to speak?
Or do you tell of your daily needs
for your up-and-coming week?
He knows all things.
He knows our wants and needs.
So, come before the King of kings
to humbly bow your knee.
He is so worthy of our praise,
He is worthy of our worship,
He is worthy of our love,
So, come face to face.

Abba Father

Abba Father,
the God of all creation.
Abba Father,
the God of every nation.
I come into the Holy Place
to fix my eyes on You.
I bow before Your throne of grace
to praise all that You do.
I bow before Your majesty
in awe of who You are.
I listen to the angels sing
how glorious You are.
"Holy, Holy, Holy!
Is the Lord God almighty."

You Are With Me

Near death experiences
have been the thing that has kept me alive.
When coward turns to courage,
when fear turns to fight,
when doubt turns into faith,
when belief becomes Your sight.
You are with me
through the brightness of the day.
You are with me
in the darkness of the night.
You are the One
that lights my path with Your glory
that shines so bright.

Arms of My Beloved

I want to rest in the arms
of my Beloved.
To sit at Your feet
and know that You are there.
I want to be covered by Your feathers
and sheltered under Your wings.
Will You breathe on me again.
Fill my life with Your love
and breathe on me again,
my Beloved.

Sweet, Sweet Wine

Your love is like a
sweet, sweet wine.
The taste so sweet
it blows my mind.
Your love is a sweet wine,
unending, unchanging.
Your love is pure.
It's Your love that
makes me whole.

REASSURANCE

Hidden Gems

"Come sit with Me,"
I heard the Lord say.
"No need to rush
your way through this day.
Look round, what do you see?
Take notice of the things you see.
There are hidden gems
in every day,
but you must stop
to see them on your way.
Take the time to see the little things,
oh, the joy those gems can bring."

The Key

Your Word says
on earth as it is in Heaven
and Your word never changes.
Everything You've spoken
is always the same.
Your Word is forever,
always to remain.
Your Word is full of promises
for everyone to see.
We only have to receive it
to unlock the mysteries.
You put in little secrets
and hidden treasures too.
We need to read the Word to find them
and spend some time with You!
That is the one, true key.

Wake Up

Wake up My beloved,
wake up My bride.
Your Saviour is here
to walk by your side.
Arise My bride,
your Beloved has come,
and we can be together as one.
Come My love,
our dance has begun.
Now, you will become one with the Son.

High Places

We're going to the high places,
will you come with Me?
Will you walk by faith
and not by what you see?
Will you choose to follow,
and surrender all you see?
I am Yours, and you are Mine,
and I will love you
until the end of time.
So, hold on My beloved,
hold onto Me.

In His Time

Father God,
the maker of all things,
made man in His image
and entrusted us to live on this earth.
To do the best we can
with the time we have.
He gave us His precious Son,
the Saviour of the world,
and His Holy Spirit,
our Comforter,
our helper in all things.
So, we can surrender
our lives into His hands.
And remain in the peace
His love brings.

Just Come

Come into the Throne Room of God,
the room full of grace.
Come in by the blood of the lamb
into the Holy Place.
Come lay down the cares of this world
and struggles of your day.
Come and let Me fill you with love
and wash the struggles away.
I will give you all you need
to help you on your way.
I will walk with you side by side
each and every day.

He Waits

Run to the Father
with arms wide open,
He loves you as you are.
There's no fear of sin or shame,
no pointing the finger
or laying the blame.
He is patient and kind,
He and holds out His hands
to give you the future
He's already planned.
There is no other love like His.
It's pure love that will never end.

Take My Hand

Come take My hand
My beautiful bride,
Let's go on a glorious ride.
The sun on our faces
and wind through our hair,
the fullness of love is in the air.
Lean back a moment
and enjoy the ride,
lean into My arms
and rest a while.
This is our moment,
this is our day
to be together in this sacred way.

Hope Comes

Lord, You come when we hit the bottom,
You are there in the hopelessness of life.
When the hole becomes too deep,
and there's no way out,
when all hope is gone,
You come.
You cover us,
You protect us,
You shield us.
You sit in the dirt
at the bottom of the hole
right beside us and hold us.
Your glory fills this place.
Your love saturates us,
and hope springs to life.

Enter His Gates

Enter His gates with thanksgiving,
with hearts so full of praise.
Come dance before Him
in the Throne Room,
and worship Jesus' name.
Down on my knees is where I will be
in worship before my King.
To surrender all I am
where my heart becomes free.
I'm in awe of You, my Saviour,
I'm in awe of Your majesty.
Here before Your Throne
I will worship Thee.

Unspoken Words

The unspoken words are the hardest to say,
when nothing seems to go the right way.
It's past emotions, hurts and pain,
a numbness and sorrow that won't go away.
No screaming or shouting or trying to blame,
just an eerie silence with no words to say.
Call out to Jesus, Gods beautiful Son.
He's faithful and able, He won't let you down.
He will lift you up
and put your feet on solid ground.
His love pours out and will fill your heart.
He will never leave you,
you will never be apart.
His love will heal you
and make you whole.
His unspoken words will be with you
until you reach your eternal home.

FATHER'S LOVE

I Am Here

Good morning My child.
I Am here.
When you wake up in the morning
and begin to start your day,
one thing I want to tell you,
one thing I want to say,
"I Am Here."
When your day gets busy
and you don't know how to cope,
one thing I want to tell you,
one thing to bring you hope,
"I Am Here."
When you start to go through storms
and you are filled with fear,
one thing I want to tell you
at the start of this new year,
"I Am Here."
When your body feels frail
and you feel you're falling apart,
one thing I want to tell you
from the depths of my heart,
"I Am Here."

Look at Me

"Look at Me."
I heard Him say.
"Close your eyes and look this way.
I want you to listen to what I say.
So, stop and listen this very day.
Every day there are mysteries
waiting to see if you can see.
Take your time and just be still
and listen to Your Fathers will.
As you spend more time with Me,
you My beloved will start to see.
So, look at Me."

God's Inheritance

We are Gods inheritance,
made in His image,
full of love and grace.
We were formed in His heart
before time began,
made in the secret place.
Every tongue and every tribe
will bow before the King.
They will give Him all the glory,
they will worship Him and sing.
To God belongs the glory
for gifting us His inheritance.

We Are His Poetry

His beloved
oh, how He loves us.
He lavishes His love
and His eyes are always on us.
His face is turned toward us,
We are His poetry.
Our conversations are written
in the book of remembrance,
which some day we will see.
We are His precious ones.
His bride,
His heavenly poetry.

You Give it All

You never give us little bits,
instead, You give it all.
You never look away
every time we call.
You never leave us on our own,
or wait for us to fall.
Your eyes are always on us,
Your heart so full of love for us all.
We are called Your beloved,
You come from Heaven above.
You notice every detail
with every child you've made.
Every single one of us
is different in some way.
We're created in Your image
full of peace, love, and grace.
You call us to come closer
to see You face to face.

IDENTITY

Roaring Like a Lion

I'm in my hospital room with three other ladies,
it's now 3:19am. I can't sleep.
There are machines beeping,
nurses coming in and out
taking blood pressures,
and giving meds. It's so busy.
My first thought of our room was,
"Oh God, these poor little ladies
sleeping without a sound."
Then there's me roaring like a lion,
Mufasa on top of his ledge,
roaring like the king He is.
We are all kings and queens,
in the kingdom of God.
We are called to walk
out on to the ledge in our region,
and roar with the authority
that God has pledged.
To let all kingdoms know
that we reign as high priests
of the living God. They will bow
down before the Lion of Judah.
The One and only King.

Come Follow Me

Jesus said,
"Come follow Me.
I'll make you fishers of men."
What was their response
of those chosen few?
They stood up and left the old
to follow the new.
They left their traditions, their families,
their old way of life,
to follow this man called Jesus Christ.
Today He still calls us,
"Come follow Me."

The Power of Your Name

At the mention of Your name
walls begin to fall.
In the middle of a storm,
You're with me through it all.
When life overwhelms me
and I start to lose my place,
You wrap Your arms around me
and cover me with Your grace.
So, I speak Your name Jesus,
in every storm I face.
You will never leave me
alone in that place.
There is freedom in Your Name.

Dare to Dream

Don't be afraid to dare to dream.
It's the birth of something amazing.
It's the seeds of the unreachable,
the seeds of the unknown,
and the seeds of the impossible.
A dream is the hope of something incredible,
it's a place where the unseen becomes visible.
Where promises are waiting to be fulfilled.
Promises of miracles,
they wait in your dreams.

TRUSTING GOD

Drawing Me Near

You're drawing me near
to a place unknown.
A place unseen and on my own.
I see You waiting for me to come
to sit and be still before Your Son.
You're drawing me into a quiet place
where I can learn to seek Your face.
Beyond the way
I've been before,
looking to You Jesus,
more and more.
"Let go of that which holds you back,
follow the long and narrow track.
With eyes closed and heart wide open,
hear the words long ago spoken."

Ride Out the Storm

It takes great courage
to ride out the storm.
It's a scary place,
a lonely place,
definitely not the norm.
The first thought is always
get out of the way.
It takes great strength
to simply stay.
Hold on to the name
of the One who saves.
The precious blood of Jesus,
He keeps us safe.
Stand your ground
and start to pray,
and command that storm to go away.
Give God the glory in all you do,
because He always has His eyes on you.
Thank you, Father,
You watch over me.
I'm safe in Your arms
even amongst the storm
and I am set free indeed.

Crossroads

Standing at the crossroad
looking all around.
Looking for directions
to the road that must be found.
Go back to the ancient path
where the way is good.
Then walk on the road
where our Saviour stood.
It is the path that's
often been misunderstood.

Trust Me and Believe

I'm looking out my window,
It's been my only view.
In the midst of all the chaos
I've learnt to follow You.
I can't cope with too much noise,
or the busyness of big crowds.
Any type of noise
always sounds so loud.
I am usually always at home,
sitting on my own.
Yet in that isolation,
I've never been alone.
My precious Holy Spirit
You've shown me how I've grown.
I hear Your gentle whispers
as You softly speak to me.
"All you need to do
is trust Me and believe."

A New Season

This is a new season,
a new start.
It's time to say yes to the things
that stir up your heart,
where your hopes begin to grow.
The Lord has filled our hearts
with treasures waiting to be found.
Gifts that He has given us
way beyond our imaginings.
For this is the day
that the Lord has made,
we shall rejoice and be glad in it.

In the Storm

Just when you think the storm has gone,
the wind picks up again.
Then you're left to wonder
if this will ever end.
The struggles in life
are sometimes hard
and you can't believe it's real.
You're left there thinking to yourself,
"Is this the real deal?"
Emotions are running high,
there's too much going on.
Scared to speak out loud
in case something else goes wrong.
Then in comes my Beloved,
He's here to save the day.
"Put your hand in Mine, My love,
and I will show you the way.
I'll put My arms around you
and cover you because You're Mine.
I'll take you to another place,
another space, and time.
To My sanctuary, My beloved,
to My home and thine.

Step Out of the Boat

Will you step out of the boat
and come to Me?
Don't look down,
keep your eyes on Me.
I Am with you in the storm,
no matter what you see.
Look up My beloved,
trust Me and believe.

SAFE PLACE

Look Up

Where do I look for my inspiration?
Where are the signs I used to see?
How will I know what You want me to do
with all there is in front of me?
I heard the Lord say,
"Don't look ahead to hear from Me,
but look up, look up for all you need.
I am always with you.
I will never leave you.
I dwell inside you,
so come deeper, My beloved,
come to Me.

You Are Always With Me

Where can I go where You can't find me?
If I go through the deepest valley,
You are with me.
If I got through trials of great sorrow,
You are with me.
If my health and state of mind
puts me on my own path,
You come with me and lead me
back to Your heart.
Your love raises me up above all harm,
and fills me with perfect peace.
You are always with me.

The Upper Room

Come to the upper room
where we can meet and pray.
A secret place,
a quiet place,
where You and I can stay.
A place that's been prepared,
a place that's set aside.
A place where my precious Jesus,
is always by my side.
A place to come and sit with Him,
and let my body rest.
A place to share my heart with Him
and lean upon His chest.

Draw Me To You

Draw me into Your heart, Jesus,
where we can be as one.
Take me into the garden
where my journey first begun.
Take me with You Jesus
from the toils of this land,
and take me to the river
where I can soak, and I can mend.
Life seems so unsure
with its highs and its lows.
It seems to race by quickly
swaying to and fro.
Deep into Your loving arms
is where I will go.
Draw me Lord to You.

Shelter of His Wings

When you feel the heat of the fire
that comes from life's troubles,
run to the Father
and stay under the shadow of the Almighty.
You will be covered and protected.
You will find shelter
with Jesus our beloved.
Abide under the shadow of the Almighty.
Run to God
where there is safety
and security.
Stay under the shelter of His wings.

Wait in My Arms

I am drawn deeper to Your presence.
I am drawn into Your Secret Place.
I come before Your throne
to seek You face to face.
I am hidden in Your love
in that most Holy Place.
Lord, You alone are my peaceful sanctuary,
my refuge, my safe place.
I'm hidden in the shelter
of Your love,
Your mercy and Your grace.
Father, I claim Your Word and declare,
"Surely your goodness
and Your mercy
shall follow me all the days of my life."

WORSHIP

Holy, Holy, Holy!

Don't be in a hurry
when you go before the King,
take the time to rest in Him
and let your praises sing.
Sit down in His presence,
to hear the angels sing.
"Holy, Holy, Holy,
is the risen King!"

Enter The Throne Room

Enter His Throne Room,
His Throne Room of grace.
Come worship God
in this sacred place.
A sea of glass
that's crystal clear,
a brilliant light
shines everywhere.
Holy God
with love so pure,
who reigns on high
forevermore.

The Trinity

To Him who sits upon the throne,
the Lord God Almighty.
To Him who sits by His side,
the spotless lamb, Jesus Christ.
To Him who is our comforter,
the beautiful Holy Spirit.
Be blessing, and honour,
and glory forever and ever.
Amen.

Your Sanctuary

Where your sanctuary is,
Your presence is also.
Draw me into the Holy Place
that brings me to my knees,
to sit before You, my Saviour,
and let me worship at Your feet.
Surrounded by amazing love
that only You can bring,
my heart breaks out in worship
to You my heart will always sing.

Dance On Coals of Fire

Falling on my knees
to worship You, my King.
To come before Your throne
and be completely free.
To dance on the coals of fire
and know that You love me.
My heart becomes full of adoration,
in love, I worship Thee.

Sanctuary of Love

Mountains so high
and valleys so low,
down on my knees is where I go.
I surrender all
that is in my heart,
and wait for You to set my path.
Lead me Jesus
and I will follow.
Call me Lord,
and I will come.
Fill my heart with Your pure love.
Your love is always enough.
Take me to our garden
where beauty is everywhere,
and love abounds forever.
Where the Your unspoken words
fill my heart,
to walk with You again
in our sanctuary of love.

DECLARATION

Here to Stay

I'm here in your morning,
I'm here in your day.
I'm here when you're tired,
and you've lost your way.
I will never leave you,
I will never walk away.
I will always be with you,
I Am here to stay.

What's in a Name?

What's in a name?
It's everything to do with you.
It's your family identity,
your past, present, and future.
It's your genealogy,
it's your culture,
and your ethnicity.
It's the lineage of your people,
and where you've come from.
From eternity to eternity.

Rise Up My Watchmen

Watchmen, watchmen,
what do you see?
Keep your eyes open
and look out for Me.
Watch for the mysteries
that have been foretold.
Watch for the signs
about to unfold.
Look and see
beyond your sight.
Watch Me come
in power and might.
This is a time to stay awake,
when the things of the world
will start to shake.
The remnant is rising to the call,
the sound of the Lord will go out to all.
Rise up My faithful ones,
My steadfast daughters,
My mighty sons.
Rise up, My watchmen,
and rise to the call.

Seeds of Destiny

You are the seeds of destiny.
Before I formed you,
I knew you.
My eyes saw your unformed body.
You were woven together
in the depths of the earth.
You were made in the secret place.
I set you apart
before you were born.
I chose you before
the foundation of creation.
Your days are written in the book.
You were born in love to be free,
you were born with a destiny.
Rise up My seed.

Storm Chaser

Father, You are the storm chaser,
the obstacle breaker,
the miracle maker.
Your glory lights up the darkness.
Your presence destroys
all things of this world.
At the sound of Your voice,
the universe trembles.
One word spoken by You
and it comes into being.
You hold all things
in the palm of Your hands.
We are Your thoughts
spoken into existence.
You made us from dust
and breathed life into us.
You are the storm chaser
You have changed us
and called us Your own.

Draw The Line

I saw a line being drawn on the sand
and heard "Thus Far And No More."
There is a battle coming
especially for our families
and our children.
Time to put on your armour
and get ready to battle.
The battle belongs to the Lord.
We win it on our knees
before the King of Glory
who's already won the victory.

I Am

I am God.
I Am the Alpha and the Omega.
I Am the beginning and the end.
I Am the first and the last.
I Am the bread of life.
I Am the light in the darkness.
I Am the way maker.
I Am the miracle worker.
I Am the promise.
I Am the Only Son of the living God.
I Am the saviour of the world,
and I Am yours.

Tell Me Your Story

Tell Me your story, My beloved,
and I'll tell You Mine.
It's been told throughout the ages,
to the end of time.
A story of love,
of hope, of mercy, and grace.
A story created in the Holy Place.
The love of the Father,
the love of His Son,
the love of His people
that's made us one.
So, tell me your story,
And I'll tell you Mine.

Come Walk With Me

Come walk with Me.
Come follow My lead.
Come trust Me and believe
for everything you need.
I Am your creator.
I Am your healer.
I Am your saviour.
I Am your Father.
I Am.

GRATITUDE

He's a Loving Father

I'm sitting in the dark,
all the lights are off,
and everyone's asleep.
I'm thanking My Father that He is my light.
He puts my feet steadily on the path
He sets before me.
I'm filled with gratitude, and thankfulness,
for His amazing love.
I'm in awe of His goodness,
His relentless love that He pours.
In the storms of my life,
and there have been many,
He's faithfully pulled me up.
It's where I'm safe and secure in Him
and where He's filled my cup.
It's been in the darkest times,
where He's been the brightest.
He saves me, He speaks to me,
He shows me things I can't explain.
I know that He hears our hearts,
He longs to have our full attention.
He's so faithful, so patient, and so gentle.
This love of our Father is so pure.

Early in the Morning

Early in the morning
before the dawn awakes,
the silence of the early hours
begins to stir in place.
I hear every movement
as the staff begin their day.
The lights are coming on
as they need to find their way.
What kind of day awaits ahead
as the staff arrive to make each bed?
I come to You, Lord Jesus,
at this new break of dawn,
and thank You that You're with me
at the break of each new morn.
This new day is Yours
to do with as You will,
and I will rest in You
and learn to be still.

Moved By Your Love

Father, we have no idea
what Your saving grace looks like.
We have no idea
what level or length
You would go to save us.
My heart is moved
at the power of Your love.
My life is changed
because of it.
There are no words to explain
how truly grateful I am.
Move me by Your love.

BE STILL

Seasons For Waiting

This is a season for waiting
that's not easy to accept.
When there seems to be no answer,
He asks, "Will you trust Me anyway?"
It's a time to stop and be still,
to come before the Lord
and listen to His will.
"For I Am God who hears your heart,
I will give you all you need,
just come to Me and wait."

Be Still and Know

Be still and know that I Am God.
Wait, and in the waiting I will come.
Worship with a pure heart
and I will open every door
and change your life
forever more.
Be still and know
that I am God.

Did You Love Well?

When you face life or death situations,
all the little things fall away.
What comes to my mind
is what will my Father say?
"Did you love well?
What did you do with My Son?
What did you do with the gifts I gave you,
My precious one?"
What can my reply be but
"Forgive me, Father, I did not!"
Life is too short to worry
about the little things in life.
He provides all we need.
He lavishes His love on us,
so don't worry about the little things!
Our Father in Heaven loves us so much.
He gave His one and only Son
to die for our sins so we can be saved,
and come back into a relationship with Him.
Love God with all your heart,
love His Son and follow Him.
Be a good steward with the gifts
God has given you. Love well.

You Know Us

You know our deepest thoughts,
our most precious desires,
our hearts.
You know our struggles and our fears,
You know everything about us.
Yet You wait for us,
You long for us
to give you even a moment.
Your heart is pouring out,
Your incredible love,
is awaiting a home,
where You can bless us
and we are known.

THE END

If you purchased this book on Amazon, would you consider leaving a review so more people can find it online?
Could you leave a review on GoodReads too?
If you purchased the book directly, please send me an email.
I'd love to hear from you and get your feedback. Thank you.

About the Author

Charmaine is of Māori descent. Her tribe is Te Arawa, her hapū is Ngāti Pikiao, her mountain is Matawhaura, and her river is the Kaituna.

Charmaine's grandfather was Te Mata-O-Hoturoa Morehu, one of the Te Arawa chiefs until his death in 1990. She is a chieftain's daughter of earth and of Heaven. Charmaine's parents, Henare and Diana Morehu, were incredibly industrious, loving people. They were hunter gatherers, and both had a competitive nature that always boasted of the best shot, the greatest catch, and the cleanest kill.

Her mother had a strong catholic faith and taught her family to pray to the Lord Jesus about everything. This gave her a foundation of faith.

Charmaine has five siblings. Her sister, Mericia, was the first in the family to become a Christian and she quickly became radically in love with Jesus. It took 10 years of praying, crying, and praying some more, before the rest of her family surrendered to Jesus' passionate love. She did not give up, even when they rejected the love of God and His saving grace. All of Charmaine's family now believe.

She has been married to the love of her life, Tata Takai, for 44 years. He is devoted to his family and has been a brilliant provider and faithful husband and friend. Charmaine has been blessed with six wonderful children and nine beautiful grandchildren.

Through the years, Charmaine has tried her hand at many crafts like classical piano, saxophone, guitar, crocheting, weaving flax and Kakahu, making jewellery, Kawakawa Balm, and now poetry. Many of her crafts she gives away.

That is who she is.

Acknowledgements

To my husband Tata, for believing that this book would one day become a reality, long before I did. For always supporting me and encouraging me to carry on. Thank you so much, my love.

To my children, my sons that live in Australia, my daughter Tasha, TJ, Isaac, Ezra, Ethan, and Samuel. Thank you for encouraging me and believing in me. For always checking in to see how I'm doing and how the book's going. Thank you, my darlings. Thank you for always having me and dad in your hearts.

To my dear friend /Author Angela Curtis, who's been right beside me helping me with the things that were beyond me. You have been amazing. This book will still be on my shelf if it wasn't for the Lord bringing you into my life to do what you do best. I will be forever grateful. Thank you, my beautiful friend.

To Judy Abraham, thank you for the countless hours of helping me to transfer my poems from phone to laptop, and doing the first lot of editing. Thank you, Judy, you're such a blessing.

To Rebecca, who changed my way of writing poetry, and who changed my way of thinking about my identity and helping me to edit and have fun through it all. Thank you.

To Maria, for taking me to all the places I couldn't drive to and doing it with so much love. Thank you.

To my amazing siblings, Margaret, Helen, Mericia, Henare, and Roy. Thank you for praying for me, for believing this was God, and for encouraging me throughout the process. For reminding me constantly that Gods got me, and God has this book. For loving me through it all. Forever grateful. Thank you.

My sister Helen, a special thank you for finally giving in and teaching me how to get an understanding not just of the Word, but to find and fall in love with Jesus. I wouldn't have taken me on, ha-ha, but you were amazing, firm, and hard sometimes, but so good for me. You taught me how to break things down and go deeper into the Word and my walk. Thank you so much Sis. Forever grateful.

To my mum and dad, who are both with Jesus. Thank you for being such amazing and loving parents. I love you and can't wait until we meet again.

To Maggie and Pete Carrasquillo, thank you for the prophetic words you spoke over me and the encouragement you gave me to run to Jesus.

To Mama Nellie, thank you for showering me with your unconditional love and for speaking into my life. You are forever in my heart, Mama.

Connect With Charmaine

Facebook:
https://www.facebook.com/charmaine.takai.7

Email:
charmainetakai@yahoo.com

Printed in Great Britain
by Amazon